ME AND MY PONY

Looking After My Horse

Toni Webber

FRANKLIN WATTS
London · Sydney

© Aladdin Books Ltd 2002
New edition published in 2004

Produced by:
Aladdin Books Ltd
28 Percy Street
London W1T 2BZ

ISBN 0–7496–5474–0

First published in Great Britain
in 2002 by:
Franklin Watts
96 Leonard Street
London EC2A 4XD

Editor:
Harriet Brown

Designers:
Flick, Book Design & Graphics
Simon Morse

Illustrators:
James Field, Terry Riley, Stephen
Sweet and Ross Watton – SGA
Frederick St Ward

Cartoons: Simon Morse

Certain illustrations have
appeared in earlier books
created by Aladdin Books.

Printed in UAE
A CIP catalogue record
for this book is available
from the British Library.

LINDEN PARK
JUNIOR SCHOOL

Contents

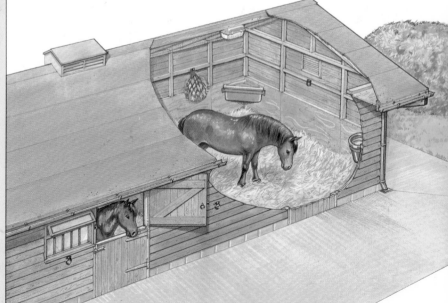

Introduction

Looking After My Horse is a lively guide to choosing a pony and taking care of its needs. There is much more to ponies than simply riding them. They need a safe place to live, the right food and tack, and importantly, they need you to look after their health. A happy, healthy and well cared-for pony is much more enjoyable to ride and spend time with, whatever activities you choose to do together.

Follow Oscar and me as we get to know each other better – and do our best not to get into too much trouble.

Always remember to...
...look in these boxes for further information about looking after your pony. They contain important points that you should try to remember.

THE RIGHTS AND WRONGS
Look out for these tick boxes, as they show you how to do things properly. Just as importantly, look out for the cross boxes. These show you how not to do things.

Q What are these boxes for?

A These question and answer panels are here to help you with any queries you may have about looking after your pony. They are on subjects relevant to the rest of the page they're on.

Follow my pony diary to find out how I get on looking after my pony. Why not make your own pony diary to keep track of your progress? It will help you remember all the fun you have and all the new friends you make as you get to know your pony.

Choosing a pony

Owning a pony is something most riders dream about. It is also a big responsibility. There are many things to consider before you choose a pony. Where should you get it from? What sort of pony should it be? Where are you going to keep it? Here are some tips to help you choose the right pony.

Arab

BUY OR LOAN?

Getting a pony on loan means you don't have to pay out a large sum of money to begin with. But its care is your reponsibility just as much as if you had bought it. Do not forget that you will have to give the pony back one day.

Native pony

WHICH PONY?

A calm pony is best if you're a nervous rider. If you are experienced, you may want a pony that is more forward going. If the pony will be living in a field all year, a native breed would be a good choice. Don't buy a pony that you will quickly grow out of, or a big horse that you plan to 'grow into'.

13hh chestnut gelding. 9yrs.
Excels XC
100% traffic, shoe, etc.
£3,000

UNDERSTANDING THE ADS

This advert tells you that the pony is a 13-hands-high, 9-year-old chestnut gelding (male). He is good at cross-country, is safe on the road and is easy to shoe. But there is a lot it doesn't say. For example, is he easy to catch? Make a list of questions to ask the seller.

Q If I find a suitable pony, should I have it vetted?

A It is usually best to get a pony vetted. There are different levels of veterinary examinations. Expensive ones are detailed and include X-rays. Cheaper ones simply tell you if the pony is fit enough for what you want it to do. Sometimes vetting shows up a problem which means that the pony is not suitable to buy.

Q Should I get my pony insured?

A Yes, you should make sure that you are covered for any damage that your pony may cause to someone else. You can also insure your pony against injury, as vet's fees can be expensive, and for the loss of, and damage to, your tack.

ACTION

The way a pony moves makes a difference to its fitness, the way it handles and how comfortable it is to ride. Ask an experienced person to look at the pony's action for you.

✔ GOOD CONFORMATION

Conformation means the way a pony is put together. The pony should look in proportion and be alert. Its eyes should be large and set well apart. Its feet should point straight ahead and its quarters should be muscular and strong.

✗ Goose rump
This is where the rump slopes steeply from the highest point of the quarters to the tail.

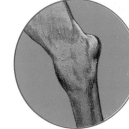

✗ Narrow chest
Its chest should be wide enough to give its heart plenty of room. But a very wide chest can cause it to be an uncomfortable ride.

✗ Capped hocks
Capped hocks look as though they are a serious fault, but they don't actually cause a problem for the pony.

quarters

✗ Splints
A splint is a bony swelling on the leg, usually below the knee. Once a splint has formed it is not a serious condition.

fetlock

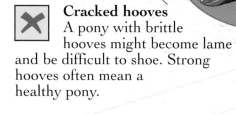

✗ Cracked hooves
A pony with brittle hooves might become lame and be difficult to shoe. Strong hooves often mean a healthy pony.

✗ Windgalls
A windgall is a soft swelling above the fetlock. This should not stop you from buying the pony as it is not a serious condition.

Always remember to...

...take a knowledgeable person with you when you go to look at a pony. Before you go, write down any questions that you need to ask. It is easy to forget questions when you get there. Try not to fall in love with the first pony you see – it is important to keep an open mind. It is a good idea to ask if you can have the pony for two weeks on a trial basis.

Saturday
We went to look at a pony today. She sounded lovely in the advert. The only thing was she turned out to be just 9 hands high. As one hand is about 10 cm, she was really much too small for me!

The stable

Wednesday
Guess what! Mum has ended up buying me Oscar – he's my favourite pony at the riding stables. I still can't believe it. We are keeping him at the riding stables as we don't have a stable or field of our own. It means getting up really early so that I can do his stable before school, but it's worth it.

A stable is useful but not vital in the care of your pony. If you do stable your new pony, you should make sure that the stable is warm, light and well drained.

STABLE FITTINGS

The stable should be on level ground and have a split door so that your pony can look out. The roof should overhang the front of the stable to protect your pony from the weather. Windows need to have bars over them and it is best to have a floor made of concrete, with a built-in drain. Any lights must be out of reach of your pony.

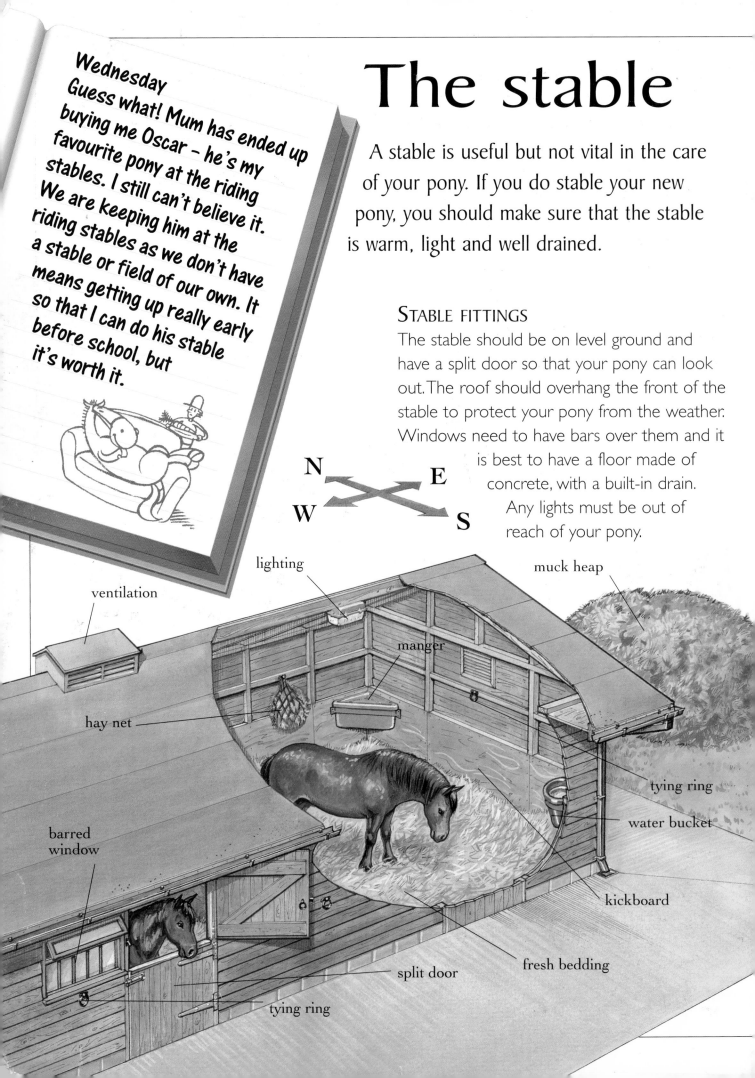

ventilation

lighting

muck heap

N
E
W
S

manger

hay net

tying ring

water bucket

barred window

kickboard

fresh bedding

split door

tying ring

LAYING BEDS AND MUCKING OUT

1 Every day, take all the droppings and wet bedding out of the stable using a fork and a skep or a wheelbarrow. If you have time, sweep all the bedding to one side to allow the floor to dry.

2 Replace the wet bedding with fresh bedding. When you lay a bed in an empty stable, use as much bedding as you can. Spread it over the floor to make a thick, soft layer. Make banks of bedding around the edges of the stable. Your pony needs less straw in the day than at night.

rake   fork

skep

wheelbarrow   broom   shovel

❶

❷

Q What is the best bedding to use?

A Straw is generally used for bedding, and wheat straw is best. Barley straw can irritate ponies with sensitive skin and they often eat oat straw. Wood shavings are the next best thing, but you must make sure there are no sharp splinters in it. Sawdust can be used with wood shavings but it is dusty and can clog up drains. Shredded paper is popular as it is warm and dust-free. But it is also heavy when damp and some ponies are allergic to the ink in the paper.

Straw

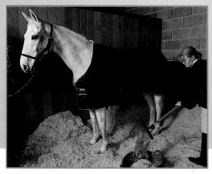

Wood shavings

Friday
I'm learning to give Oscar a really comfortable bed. At first, I didn't use enough straw. Gerry, the owner of the riding stables, had to show me how to shake it to get rid of the lumps. She made me build really thick banks of straw round the edges and I had to pat them with the back of my shovel to make them square.

Keeping a pony at grass

Ponies are grazing animals. If possible, fresh grass should always be part of their diet. Hardy, native ponies are usually healthier if they live out, even in winter. More delicate ponies should spend part of the day out in the field.

TYPES OF GRASS

Old, well-established grass is the best grazing for ponies. Lots of different grasses will have grown over the years. New grass or grass that has been fertilised could be too rich for your pony.

POISONOUS PLANTS

Some plants are poisonous to ponies. You must check that there is nothing dangerous growing in or near your field. Ask an adult to help you pull up any dangerous plants and burn them on a bonfire.

Horsetails
This weed is most often found on waste ground. It can grow in fields where the grass hasn't been properly cared for.

White snakeroot
This is mainly found in the US. It grows on the edge of woodlands. It can be got rid of by using a herbicide (chemical).

Ragwort
This weed grows on grass verges, heathland and in fields. It should be pulled up by the roots and burned.

Deadly nightshade
This plant grows mainly in wooded areas. It can be found in hedgerows and should be pulled up if it grows in or near your pony's field.

Red maple
This tree is mainly found in the US and Canada. These trees should be fenced off from your pony's field.

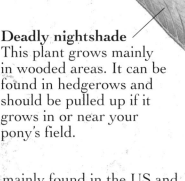

CARE OF THE PASTURE

Horses and ponies waste a lot of grass in their field. They often trample good grass and turn other areas sour with their droppings. Pick up droppings every day using a shovel and a wheelbarrow or skep. Or you could use heavy, waterproof gloves to pick up the droppings. It is a job well worth doing as it helps to keep the grass and your pony healthy.

RESTING FIELDS

If your riding stables have a lot of grazing land, it may be divided up into smaller fields. Fields that are empty for a while can be sprayed with pesticide (chemical) to get rid of parasites and weeds. Sheep or cattle can be kept in fields with ponies. This improves the quality of the grazing as sheep and cattle eat grass that ponies leave.

Bracken
This is found on moorland, heathland and in woodland. Bracken is dangerous over a long period of time as it can damage your pony's liver.

Yew
Yew trees are extremely poisonous. If your pony's field borders land where yew trees grow, it is very important to fence them off. Every part of the tree is poisonous – even the twigs.

Black locust
This is found mainly by the side of the road in the US. Your pony must not be allowed to eat it.

1 pm – Oscar was right at the far side of the field this morning. I had to trek through the mud to get him. Next week, he's going into one of the smaller paddocks so that the big field can be rested and given some fertiliser. He'll be with Annabel's pony, Daniel, so he won't get lonely.

Q Is it all right to keep my pony in a field on its own?

A Most ponies do not like to be kept on their own. They are herd animals and need company. If there aren't any other ponies to share your pony's field, you could put a few sheep, cows or even a goat in the field.

Fencing

The fence around your field must be strong and well-built. Inspect it regularly to check for any damage. It does not have to be very high, as even ponies that are good at jumping rarely try to jump out. The gate also needs to be strong and easy for you – but not your pony – to open and close.

TYPES OF FENCING

The best type of fence to use is a strongly-built, wooden post-and-rail fence. Fences with three rails are the most popular. Another popular type of fence has plain wire or plastic in place of the wooden rails. Try to avoid barbed wire and wire netting as these can be dangerous for your pony.

Post and rail
This is a safe and secure type of fence. Three rails are better than two.

Post and plastic rail
Broad plastic strips are a cheaper alternative to wooden rails. Plastic strips are better than plain wire fencing as they are more easily seen.

Rail and wire
The wire used in this type of fence must be plain, not barbed. It must also be pulled taut or your pony could get tangled in it.

Q What sort of gate is best for my pony's field?

A The best gate is a five-barred one, which swings open without touching the ground. It should have a latch that your pony cannot open. You can help look after the gate by not climbing over it or sitting on it. If you do have to climb over it, always do so at the hinge end. Your gate must be wide enough for your pony to pass through easily.

FIELD SHELTER

Most ponies don't mind bad weather as long as they have somewhere to shelter from the wind. The side of a building, a high hedge or a hollow in the ground all offer shelter. A purpose-built field shelter provides a dry place for you to tie up a hay net. In summer, your pony can use it to escape from flies and the hot sun.

prevailing wind

bedding

FIELD SECURITY

You must make sure that the gate to your field is always securely shut. Some ponies learn how to open gates, so you should fit a pony-proof latch. You could put on a padlock as a precaution against horse thieves. As a further guard, you could get your pony freeze-marked. This involves having your pony permanently marked with a number, usually on its back. If it is stolen and offered for sale, the number makes it easier for the police to know that the pony is yours.

Always remember to...

...make sure that your pony has enough to drink. If you are lucky, water will be piped to a trough. These troughs are usually controlled by a valve so that they cannot overflow. Otherwise, you will have to fill your trough regularly using a hosepipe. An old bath can be used as a water trough. Make sure that all the taps have been taken off and that there are no sharp edges for your pony to injure itself on. In the winter you must break the ice in the trough every day.

Dual system

When you have both a stable and a field, you can give your pony the best of both worlds – living in and living out. This dual system is used by many riding stables and works very well.

Winter

Always remember to...

...lay a good, thick bed, especially on winter nights. A thick bed gives your pony a comfortable resting place if it wants to lie down. Some ponies are very restless and paw at their bedding and create bare patches. All you can do is add as much bedding as you can. The day-time bed in summer does not need to be as thick as a night-time or winter bed. Your pony is less likely to lie down during the day.

HALF IN, HALF OUT

Using the dual system means that your pony spends half the time indoors and half in the field. In summer, it is best to keep your pony in the stable during the day and out in the field at night. In winter, your pony is better off in the stable at night. It can go out in the field for exercise during daylight hours.

FULL LIVERY

Full livery is when you hand the daily care of your pony over to the riding stables. The owner of the stables makes sure that it is fed, has new shoes and is wormed. Everything is done for you. It is not the most popular type of livery as you miss out on all the fun of caring for your pony.

PARTIAL LIVERY

With partial livery you agree with the owner of the stables exactly how much time you can spend looking after your pony. The staff at the riding stables will do the rest. This could mean that you exercise and muck out every day, but the staff arrange shoeing, worming and giving feeds at night.

DIY LIVERY

The cost of DIY livery covers a stable and grazing for your pony. It should also include space in a hay store for your hay and space in the feed room for your pony's feed. Everything else is your responsibility.

Summer

TACK SECURITY

Tack security is very important. Tack thefts are common and often the stolen property is not recovered. All your tack should be marked with your name or post code in permanent pen. Any other belongings that you leave at the stables – rugs, bandages, etc – should also be named. If you can, store your tack in a locked room. In some stables, security lights and guard dogs put off thieves.

Later – The tack room at our stables is a sort of double room. The inside bit is like a big walk-in cupboard. It has a lock and everyone keeps their saddles and bridles in there. We all have bridle hooks and saddle racks with our pony's name on them. The outer room is where we keep things like rugs, hats and grooming kits.

Grooming

Most ponies enjoy being groomed – some even fall asleep while you work. Grooming keeps the skin healthy and the coat shiny. Daily grooming ensures that you notice any cuts or other problems as early as possible.

stable rubber

sponges

dandy brush

hoof oil and brush

hoof pick

body brush

water brush

curry comb (metal)

sweat scraper

curry comb (rubber)

mane comb

mane-pulling comb

QUICK-RELEASE KNOT

When tying a pony up, always use a quick-release knot, as shown on the left. It will hold your pony securely. To undo the knot, remove the loose end from the loop and tug it sharply. A quick-release knot like this may be necessary if your pony gets tangled up in any way.

❶

❷

❸

PICKING OUT HOOVES

Cleaning out your pony's hooves is something you should never forget to do. Work from the back of the foot towards the toe using a metal hoof pick. Pay special attention to the grooves on each side of the centre 'V' of the foot, called the frog.

Grooming kit
To make sure you don't lose any items in your grooming kit, you should keep them all together in a grooming box. If your pony is at a livery stable, write your name or your pony's name on each piece of equipment.

Always remember to...

...attach a loop of baler twine to each metal tie ring in your stable. Tie your pony to the twine, not to the metal ring. If your pony is frightened and pulls back suddenly, the twine will break and your pony will not injure itself. Your hay net should also be tied to a baler twine loop.

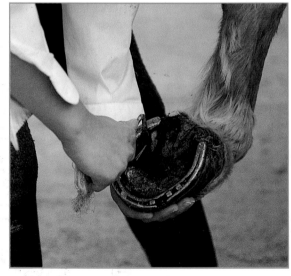

ORDER OF GROOMING

The usual order of grooming is to work from the top of the head to the hindquarters. Do this first on one side and then on the other. Use the body brush to brush the head, mane and tail. Finish off the body with the stable rubber. Sponge the eyes, nose and dock area (under the tail).

6.30 pm – I think Oscar must look for the muddiest part of the field before getting down to roll. I always seem to work harder than anyone else at getting him clean. I am just thankful that he isn't a grey. Getting rid of grass stains takes forever!

PULLING THE MANE

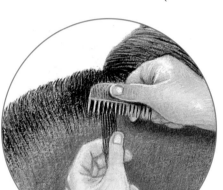

You only need to pull your pony's mane if it is very thick and untidy. The purpose is to shorten it, make it lie flat or make it easier to plait. Wrap a few hairs at a time around a comb and pull them out. Only pull the long hairs from underneath.

Q Is grooming a grass-kept pony any different from grooming a stabled pony?

A With a grass-kept pony, you can use a dandy brush directly on the coat. If your pony is very muddy, you can use a plastic or rubber curry comb on it. Take care not to groom a grass-kept pony too vigorously as it needs the natural grease in its coat to keep it warm and dry. Never pull a grass-kept pony's tail as it needs a full tail for protection from flies and the weather.

OILING HOOVES

Your pony will look very smart when its hooves are oiled. This is nearly always done before a show. Be careful not to oil the hooves too often. Spreading a thin film of oil over them stops them from absorbing water. This can make them brittle.

Use a dandy brush to remove mud from a grass-kept pony.

Use a body brush or an old, soft dandy brush on the tail; never use a mane comb.

Use separate, differently coloured sponges for the head and dock areas.

Pick out your pony's feet every day.

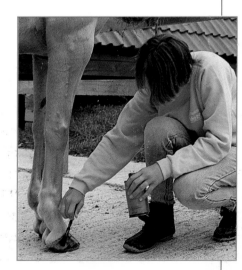

Tack

There are so many different items of tack that you may find it difficult to know what is best for your pony. Always ask for help from someone who really understands what each item is used for. It is very important to look after your tack properly.

Q How often should I clean my tack?

A If you want to be a perfectionist, the answer is every time you use it. This is unrealistic, but you should aim to clean it once a week. It helps if you can rinse the bit and wipe mud from the tack after every ride. Inspect your saddle and bridle for damage each time you clean them.

TYPES OF GIRTH

The most popular girth is made of synthetic fabric and has a soft, strong filling. Other girths are made from leather, webbing or string. Leather girths need a lot of care to keep them supple. String girths can pinch your pony.

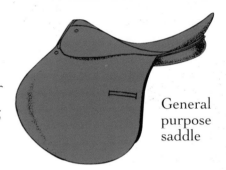

General purpose saddle

STIRRUP IRONS

Stirrup irons should be made from stainless steel. They must be large enough to leave about 1 cm clear on either side of your boot at its widest part. If they are bigger, your whole foot could slip through. If they are smaller, your foot could get stuck.

Plain iron

Simplex safety iron

Safety iron

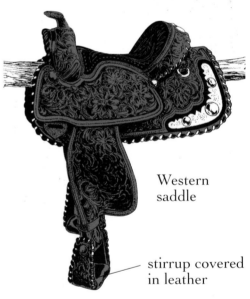

Western saddle

stirrup covered in leather

Always remember to...

...make sure that the hairs on your pony's back lie the right way under the saddle. To do this, place the saddle well up on the withers and push it back into place. If you use a numnah (a cloth under the saddle), it should be slightly bigger than the saddle and must not press on the pony's backbone.

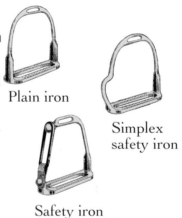

withers

numnah

TYPES OF SADDLE

General purpose saddles are the most widely used. These are usually made of leather and are shaped to encourage the rider to sit in a balanced position. Western saddles are very comfortable for both the rider and the pony.

PUTTING ON THE BRIDLE

The main purpose of the bridle is to hold the bit in the correct position in your pony's mouth. The browband holds the headpiece in place behind your pony's ears. The cheekpieces can be adjusted to raise or lower the bit in the mouth. The throatlash, which is part of the headpiece, prevents the bridle from coming off. The reins link the rider to the bit. Always loop the reins over your pony's neck when you put the bridle on.

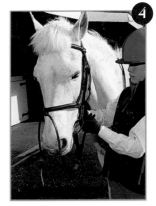

Hold the headpiece with your right hand. Lift it to the level of your pony's ears. Give the bit to your pony with your left hand.

As soon as the bit is in your pony's mouth, put the headpiece over its ears.

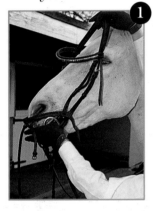

Do up the throatlash. There should be room for one hand's width between it and your pony's jawbone.

Do up the noseband. You should be able to insert two fingers between it and your pony's face.

Pelham bridle

NOSEBANDS

A simple noseband (a cavesson) is just for show as it is not needed to keep the bridle on. A drop noseband is used to stop a pony from opening its mouth so wide that the bit has no effect. Grakle nosebands work in the same way as a drop noseband. They have two nosebands, which cross over at the front.

Drop noseband

Grakle noseband

TYPES OF BIT

The most common bit is the jointed snaffle. It presses on the corners of the mouth and the tongue. A curb bit has a curb chain. Pressure on the reins causes the curb chain to tighten in the chin groove to make your pony bring its nose in. A Pelham bit uses the actions of a curb bit and a snaffle bit.

Jointed snaffle bit

Pelham bit

curb chain

Curb bit

Mum bought me some second-hand stirrup leathers. They've been looked after so well that they're lovely and soft!

Friday

Oscar is so greedy I'm surprised he doesn't get a tummy ache. He always finishes his feed before any of the other ponies. I am now adding more chaff to his feed to make him take a bit longer over eating it. So far it seems to be working. Annabel's pony, Daniel, finished first today.

Feeding

In the wild, horses and ponies find their food wherever they can. They cover large areas of land as they search for food. The food they find is very varied – from sweet meadow grasses to the leaves and bark of trees. The variety gives them all the vitamins and minerals they need to stay healthy. Your pony relies on you to control its diet.

Q What is hard food ?

Chaff and molasses meal

A Hard food is another name for concentrated food. Oats are the best all-round food but may be too rich for some ponies. Barley is less rich than oats and is very useful for ponies that lose weight easily. Cubes (pellets) or mixed food can be given instead of the actual grain. In both cases, the manufacturer uses different grains and a careful balance of vitamins and minerals in the feed. Ask an experienced person to help you choose the right feed for your pony.

Corn

Bran

Barley

Dried alfalfa

Grass

Hay

BULK FEED

The basis of a pony's diet is bulk food, such as grass and hay. The choice of any additional food you give your pony depends on the work it does and the type of pony it is. A very active pony needs a diet made up of 60% bulk food and 40% hard food. A pony that is out in a field as a break from normal work needs a diet of just bulk food. Ask an experienced person what the balance should be for your pony.

Winter feeding

	8.00 am	12 noon	4.00 pm	8.00 pm
14 hh pony Weighs 375 kg. Mainly stabled. Hacking with some jumping. 9.375 kg feed per day	1 kg hard food 2 kg hay	No hard food 1 kg hay	2.125 kg hard food No hay	No hard food 3.25 kg hay
12 hh pony Weighs 300 kg. In at night, out during the day. Light hacking. 7.5 kg feed per day	No hard food 2 kg hay	No hard food No hay	1 kg hard food 1 kg hay	No hard food 3.5 kg hay

Summer feeding

	8.00 am	12 noon	4.00 pm	8.00 pm
14 hh pony Weighs 375 kg. Stabled during day, out at night. Very active. 9.375 kg food per day	2 kg hard food 3 kg hay	No hard food No hay	1.125 kg hard food No hay	Grass makes up the rest of the daily food
12 hh pony Weighs 300 kg. Out all the time. Light hacking, some shows. 7.5 kg food per day	1 kg hard food No hay	Grass for the rest of the daily food	Grass for the rest of the daily food	Grass for the rest of the daily food

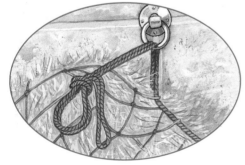

HAY

The most usual hay for horses is meadow hay. Alfalfa (lucerne) is similar to hay. It contains lots of calcium, so ponies fed on alfalfa need a smaller amount of hard food. You should feed hay in a hay net that is tied with a quick-release knot.

FEED QUANTITY

The chart above gives you an idea of what to feed two ponies of different heights and living arrangements. No two ponies are the same. Some put on weight much more easily than others. Whatever your feeding routine, you must always provide fresh water for your pony.

I still can't believe how much water Oscar can drink – especially when we come back from a fast ride!

Tack and feed rooms

Tack is valuable and should be cared for properly. Regular cleaning is only one part of its treatment. The way it is stored is also important. In a well-run livery stables, the tack room sometimes feels like a meeting place when everyone is in there looking after their tack.

I have put some extra hooks up next to my saddle rack for my spare stirrup irons. They may come in useful one day.

Saddle racks
Saddle racks are designed to fit any size of saddle. They have a hook underneath for spare stirrup leathers or girths.

Bridle hooks
A bridle hook should be wide enough to allow the headpiece to bend naturally over it.

Hay nets
Spare hay nets can be kept in the tack room if there is enough room for them.

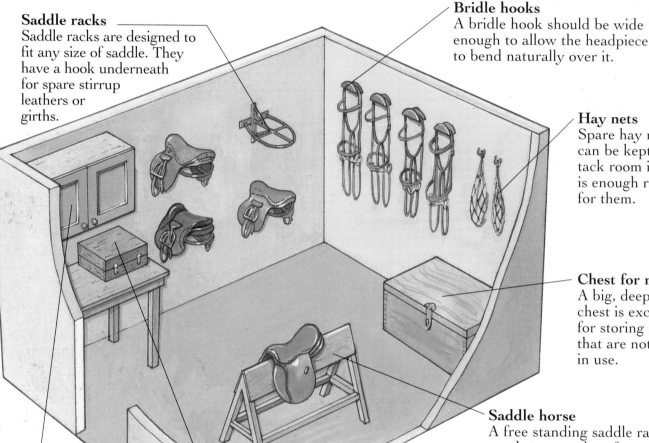

Chest for rugs
A big, deep, dry chest is excellent for storing rugs that are not in use.

Saddle horse
A free standing saddle rack is a good storage place for a spare saddle until it is provided with its own rack.

Medicine cupboard
A basic veterinary cupboard should contain antiseptic solution, non-adhesive dressings, a roll of sticky tape, scissors, a poultice and clean cotton wool.

Grooming box
Most ponies have their own grooming kit. A kit normally contains dandy, body and water brushes, a curry comb, hoof pick, sponges and a stable rubber.

TACK ROOM
It is amazing how much equipment one pony can have. It is best to store your saddle on a shaped rack. Only store one saddle per rack. Your bridle should be kept on a proper bridle hook. Nails are good for storing girths, stirrup leathers and head collars.

HANDLING AND CARRYING TACK

Treating your saddle carelessly could damage it. Inside a saddle is a framework called a tree. If you drop the saddle, you could break the tree. Trees cannot be mended. To carry your saddle, let it rest over your forearm. Loop the bridle over your shoulder, with the reins caught up by the throatlash. Never let the reins drag on the ground. Clean your tack regularly with saddle soap and a little water.

STORAGE OF HAY

Hay should be stored in a proper haystore or barn. This protects it from the weather. The hay bales should be stacked on wooden pallets to keep them off the ground and to allow air to circulate. If you have to store them outdoors, you must put a waterproof cover over them that cannot blow off.

Q What should be kept in a feed room?

A The feed room should contain feed buckets, a wooden spoon for stirring, scoops for measuring and scales for weighing. Hard food should be kept in vermin-proof bins with lids. Each type of food should be kept in a separate bin and be labelled clearly. Vegetables should be stored off the ground.

Monday
I decided to clean out my grooming box because it was in a real mess. Some hoof oil had been spilt and it was all mixed up with plaiting bands and an old hairnet I thought I'd lost. It took me half an hour to clean the box properly. Oscar won't even notice!

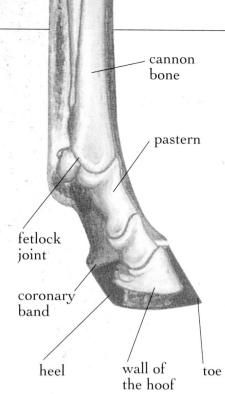

cannon bone

pastern

fetlock joint

coronary band

heel

wall of the hoof

toe

Feet and shoes

There is a saying, 'No foot, no horse,' and this is very true. A pony's feet need special care if it is to be healthy and capable of work. Hooves grow all the time, like fingernails. A good farrier will make sure that your pony has healthy feet and shoes that fit properly. Shoes stop your pony's feet from wearing down too fast when it is ridden on hard surfaces.

THE FOOT

Underneath your pony's foot you will see a soft V-shape, which extends from the heel towards the toe. This is the frog. It absorbs shock and improves the circulation of blood in the foot. The bars and the wall of the hoof give the foot strength. Your pony has no feeling in this part of its hoof, so it does not hurt your pony to have nails put in to keep the shoes on.

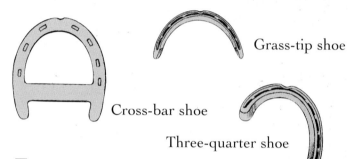

Grass-tip shoe

Cross-bar shoe

Three-quarter shoe

TYPES OF SHOE

Horseshoes are made of iron and have a groove in them to stop the pony slipping. Cross-bar shoes and three-quarter shoes are used on ponies with damaged feet. Grass-tip shoes are used on horses living out and not being ridden, to give protection to the front part of the foot.

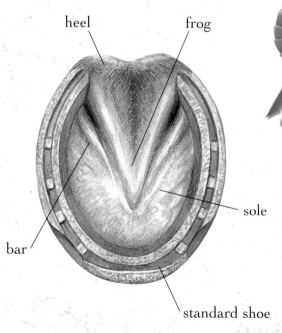

heel

frog

sole

bar

standard shoe

Always remember to...

...check and clean out your pony's feet every day. You need a hoof pick to remove mud and stones that get packed into the hollows between the frog and the wall. Use the hoof pick from the heel to the toe of each foot in turn. Sweep up the pickings afterwards. You can paint the outside of the hoof with hoof oil to make your pony's feet look smart. It is a good idea to carry a hoof pick in your pocket when out riding. You never know when you might need it.

FOOT PROBLEMS

Some foot problems can be solved by changing your pony's diet. Others need the attention of a good farrier. Sand cracks are cracks that run down

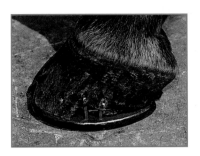

from the top of the hoof. They are a serious condition. Grass cracks run upwards from the ground and are less serious. If you are unsure of what to do about a foot problem, ask your farrier for advice.

healthy foot

grass cracks

Q How often should I call the farrier?

A You will need to call the farrier every four to eight weeks. Check your pony's shoes daily. If the hoof wall sticks out over the shoe, the foot needs trimming. Other signs that your pony needs new shoes include: the shoes clicking, your pony stumbling a lot, clenches (risen nails) sticking up from the wall of the hoof, thin shoes and loose shoes.

TYPES OF STUD

There are two types of stud – the road stud and the competition stud. Both give your pony extra grip. Studs are only used in the hind shoes. Road studs are shallow with a hard tip. Competition studs are pointed, for use in hard, dry conditions, or large and square, for use in mud.

Road stud   Competition stud

7 pm – The farrier came today to give Oscar a new set of shoes. I asked if it would be a good idea to leave his shoes off altogether. He wasn't keen, as we do ride on the road sometimes. He said that if I decided not to have shoes, Oscar's feet would still need trimming regularly to keep them in good shape.

Health check

Your pony cannot tell you if it is feeling ill. It is up to you to recognise signs of sickness and be ready to treat them or call a vet. Luckily, most horses and ponies remain healthy and are usually fit and active well into old age.

HEAD CHECK

A healthy pony's eyes are wide open and bright. Its ears should be pricked and it should be alert. The nostrils should be free from discharge. Breathing should be quiet and even. If your pony is sick, it will seem listless and dull-eyed. It will show little interest in its surroundings. There could be discharge from its eyes or nose.

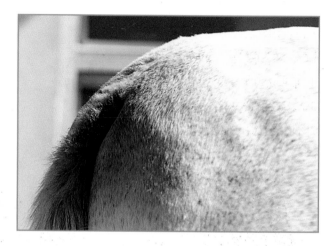

COAT CHECK

A healthy pony has a sleek, flat coat and supple skin. Ponies can get a condition called sweet itch (above). They get so itchy that they can rub all the hair from their tail or mane. If your pony's coat is dull and it seems to be sweating, then there may be something wrong. If there is no experienced person around to advise you, always call the vet.

3 pm – Oscar seemed a bit lame today. When we looked him over, we couldn't find anything wrong. His legs weren't hot or swollen and he hadn't got a stone in his shoe. He must have trodden on something sharp. We're going to give him a rest tomorrow and see how he is the next day.

Always remember to...

...check for saddle or girth galls if your pony is overweight or has not been ridden for a while. These are small, painful swellings on the skin that form under the saddle and girth. This mainly happens in the spring when ponies eat lots of new grass and put on weight. The condition is made worse by badly-fitting or dirty tack. If the skin is broken, bathe it gently in a weak antiseptic solution. Do not use the saddle on the pony until the sores have completely healed.

Q Do I need to vaccinate my pony?

A Yes. Vaccination will protect your pony against equine flu and an illness called tetanus. You may not be able to go to some shows and competitions without a valid vaccination certificate.

GENERAL HEALTH

Ponies are generally healthy and are rarely ill. If a pony is limping, the cause is most likely to be in the foot, but you should check the lower legs for heat or swelling. You can apply a poultice to reduce swelling, but lameness usually improves with rest.

Later Oscar had his flu jab today. It was really amazing. The vet just patted him on the neck, talking to him all the time, and the next thing I knew he was screwing a syringe into the needle that was sticking into Oscar's neck. I don't think Oscar felt a thing.

Listlessness
This is a sign that something is wrong. Your pony will hang its head. Its eyes and coat will look dull. It will have no interest in what is going on.

Lameness
Check that nothing is stuck in the foot. Rest is the best cure for lameness.

Off feed
This could mean your pony has an internal problem. Drinking much more water than normal can also mean that something is wrong.

TEETH CHECK

Your pony's teeth continue to grow throughout its life. The front teeth are used to pull grass or hay. The back teeth grind the food before it is swallowed. Sometimes, the teeth develop sharp edges. Occasionally a back tooth will grow so long that it damages the tongue and the inside of the cheeks. Your pony should have a regular visit from the horse dentist so that its teeth can be rasped (have sharp edges removed).

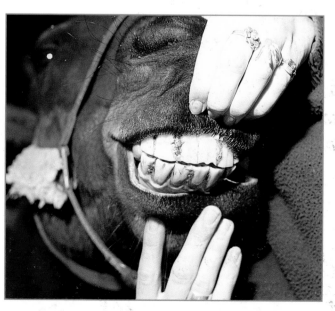

Moving on

It is a sad day when you realise that you have grown too big for your pony, especially if you have had it for a long time. It is best if it can go on to someone else who can have as much fun as you have had.

Wednesday
Somebody asked me what I'm going to do when I grow out of Oscar. What a horrible thought! Luckily, it's not going to happen for years and years – so I'm not even going to think about it. Well, I suppose I could pass him on to Annabel's little sister – eventually.

FROM PONY TO HORSE
It is not easy to know when you have grown too big for your pony. You may not feel too big, but your legs and your body become too long. You and your pony will no longer feel balanced. Building up a relationship with a new horse can take a long time, but it is worth the effort.

RETIREMENT

An old pony may not be very agile or fast but it can still easily carry children on it's back. The ideal retirement for a pony is for it to remain in familiar surroundings with its old companions. It can still do a little regular work to keep fit.

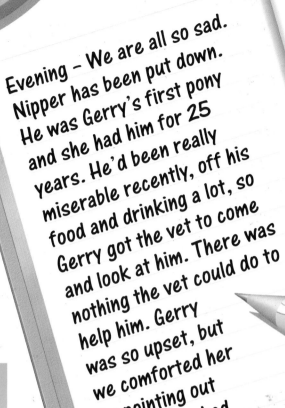

Evening – We are all so sad. Nipper has been put down. He was Gerry's first pony and she had him for 25 years. He'd been really miserable recently, off his food and drinking a lot, so Gerry got the vet to come and look at him. There was nothing the vet could do to help him. Gerry was so upset, but we comforted her by pointing out that Nipper had a wonderful life.

Q What choices do I have when I outgrow my pony?

A You could put your pony out on loan. If it is a good pony, there will be no shortage of volunteers. You may have to sell your pony in order to buy a new one. Don't worry, it can be just as happy in its next home as it was with you. If you have a younger brother or sister, you could pass your pony on to him or her.

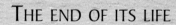

THE END OF ITS LIFE

Some horses and ponies live well into their twenties, thirties or even forties. However, it is not kind to prolong the life of a pony that is constantly in pain. If your pony is no longer enjoying life then it should be put to sleep. It is kinder and more humane for this to be done at home in familiar surroundings. Your vet will advise you of the best method and will carry it out with sympathy and understanding.

Quiz time

Can you remember what you have learned in this book? Why not test yourself and your friends by having a go at this quiz?

Always remember to...

...think about how your pony feels. Ponies can be stubborn, but if your pony is refusing to do what you want, it could be that it is uncomfortable or in pain. Check that your tack fits well, that you are feeding it the right food and that it hasn't injured itself. By taking care of your pony, you will have more fun with each other.

I What name is given to each of the following?
  a A steeply sloping rump
  b A soft swelling just above the fetlock
  c A bony swelling below the knee

2 Name four types of bedding.

3 What do we call:
  a The fleshy V-shaped section on the bottom of the foot?
  b The cloth that goes under the saddle?
  c The tools used for getting mud off a field-kept pony?

4 Name four poisonous plants.

5 Name four types of rug.

6 What are:
  a Brushing boots?
  b Over-reach boots?
  c Travelling boots?

7 Give four signs of illness.

8 Name two types of noseband that are used to stop a pony from opening its mouth too wide.

Useful addresses

The Pony Club
The Pony Club HQ
NAC
Stoneleigh Park
Kenilworth
Warwickshire
CV8 2RW
Tel: 01327 361 388
www.pony-club.org.uk

Association of British
Riding Schools
Queens Chambers
38–40 Queen Buildings
Queen Street
Penzance
Cornwall
TR18 4HB
Tel: 01736 69440

Saturday
I've been thinking it's about time Oscar and I got a bit more ambitious. I might enter some shows with him next summer. Gymkhana games would be fun!

Answers

1 a Goose rump b Windgall c Splint 2 Straw, shavings, sawdust, shredded paper 3 a Frog b Numnah c Dandy brush and a curry comb 4 Choose from yew, ragwort, bracken, acorns, horse tail, deadly nightshade, black locust, white snakeroot 5 New Zealand rug, sweat rug, summer sheet, day rug 6 a Wrap-around leg guards b Bell-shaped rubber boots that fit over the front feet c Leg wraps, usually made of quilted material, that reach from above the knee or hock to the hoof 7 Listlessness, sweating, off feed, discharge from nostrils 8 Drop noseband, grakle noseband

Glossary

alfalfa (lucerne)
A plant used for making hay, also known as lucerne. It is very rich in calcium.

bars
Ridges underneath the hoof on either side of the frog.

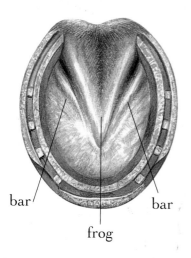

bar / bar
frog

clenches
Horseshoe nails after they have passed through the hoof and the tops of them have been twisted off.

coronary band
The top of the hoof from which the horn of the hoof grows.

dock
The area under a pony's tail.

farrier
A trained person who takes care of a pony's feet and fits new shoes.

frog
The V-shaped part of the underneath of the hoof. It absorbs shock.

gelding
A male horse or pony that is suitable for riding. A female is called a mare.

girth
The strap that holds the saddle in place on a pony.

hands
Horses and ponies are measured in hands. It is a unit of measurement that is roughly the width of an adult's hand. One hand is equal to 10 cm.

livery
The name given to the practice of keeping a pony at stables that aren't your own. You pay a fee to the owner of the stables.

rasping
When a vet removes sharp edges from the teeth of a pony.

skep
A container used to collect dirt and droppings that have been picked up from a stable or field.

studs
Metal bolts that screw into a pony's shoes to give it extra grip on slippery ground.

sweet itch
A severe skin condition that affects the top of the tail and the crest of the neck. The pony gets very itchy and can rub off all its hair.

trough
A large container used to hold drinking water for ponies in a field.

vetting
When a vet checks the health of a horse or pony.

withers
The projecting bone at the base of the neck. The height of a pony is measured from here.

worming
When you give a pony treatment to get rid of worms living in the pony's gut. Treatment may be a paste squirted into the mouth or a powder mixed with feed.

Index

Photo credits
Abbreviations: l-left, r-right, b-bottom, t-top, c-centre, m-middle
Front & back cover, 4ml, 7bm, 9t, 13c, 15bm, 16b, 18rc, 18rb, 18c, 18lb, 19 all, 21t top, 22br, 23c, 25ml, 25br, 26tr, 26ml, 30, 31b — Select Pictures. 1, 4tr, 5 both, 7tl, 7tr, 7bl, 8tr, 11 both, 12b, 13t, 15t, 15br, 17 all, 18rt, 18lt, 21b both, 23tl, 23b, 24 both, 26b, 27 all, 28r — Kit Houghton Photography. 3, 8ml, 9br, 10mr, 16ml both, 18bm, 28ml, 29t — Corel. 4c, 14br, 28–29, 32t, 32mr — Aubrey Wade. 25t — Redwings Horse Sanctuary.
Picture research: Brian Hunter Smart